★

FURNITURE ARRANGEMENT
AND BALANCE

★

BY CHRISTINE HOLBROOK
Associate Editor and
Home-Furnishings Director of
BETTER HOMES & GARDENS

★

An interesting furniture grouping may be achieved by cleverly placing a small table, with its reading lamp, between two chairs so that it serves them both

What Is Balance?

THE secret of the successful room lies in its atmosphere of hospitality, livableness, and comfort which is acquired by the proper use of balance and arrangement.

Furniture arrangement is fully as important if not more so than its selection; for even the simplest of furnishings, well balanced and comfortably arranged, can achieve such an effect that the average observer will remark little outside the real comfort enjoyed.

It is no simple task to move into a house and place

Formal balance each side of a fireplace
can be used with informal balance in
the rest of the room's arrangement

the furniture, purchased for other surroundings, in har-
monious relationship, one piece to another. Often the
size of the furniture, the shape of the room, provide
difficulties that can be overcome only by extreme care
and thought.

It is well here to define balance as it is used in connec-
tion with well-arranged rooms. There are two recognized
forms of balance—formal and informal. Formal balance
expresses itself with a more dignified air than informal
balance. In the accompanying illustration on this page of
two armchairs, one on either side of the fireplace, we
have a perfect example of formal balance. It is a definite

repetition on each side of a central point of interest, in this instance the fireplace.

We face a far more difficult task when we attempt to achieve informal balance. We are handling a subtle quality which requires more study and yet has all the charm of apparently being unstudied, see page 14. You will be aided in the informal balance of a room by keeping a careful proportion between heavy and light furniture, particularly in the case of heavy overstuffed pieces.

Combining Formal and
Informal Groups

Ends of rooms should balance each other not only in furnishings, but in the lighting as well. In seeking balance and arrangement of a room the large pieces of furniture should be placed first; one balancing another, then the smaller objects arranged so that they make convenient groupings as well as balanced units.

One will know if one has succeeded in balancing a room if the eye is held the same length of time by each individual grouping. You may successfully combine formal and informal grouping in the same room. It is really a perfect combination, for a little air of dignity is never amiss and serves as a foil to the intimate informal balancing. Color is an important factor in obtaining balance, often providing the necessary note to balance the arrangements on desk tops, tables, bookcases, and chests.

BEFORE attempting to arrange your furniture, it is best to draw a plan of your home showing the way in which you wish your pieces placed.

How to Correct Errors

WRONG

WRONG: The room is uninviting. Chairs have backs to doors and the davenport is askew. Height is directed to one end with an awkward effect

RIGHT: The heaviest piece is placed near the largest wall for balance. The secretary balances the bookcases. Group the chairs near the large window

KEY: (1) davenport, (2) coffee table, (3) club chair, (4) secretary and chair, (5) Cogswell chair, (6) wing chair, (7) reading table, (8) open armchair, (9) book table, (10) bookcase

RIGHT

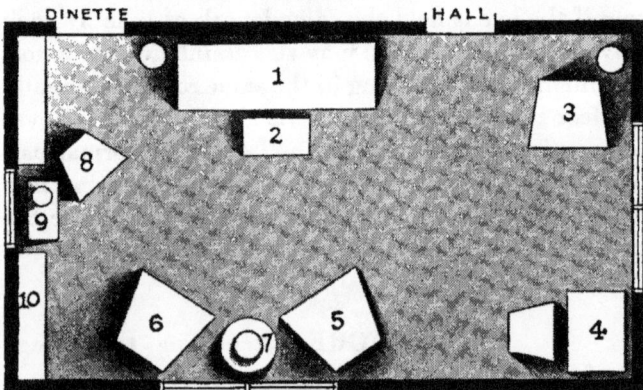

In Room Arrangement

WRONG

WRONG: The fireplace grouping is over-emphasized at the
expense of the rest of the room.
Order, repose are lost by placing desk and piano at angles

RIGHT: Here the same furniture is arranged harmoniously.
The windows are featured and
near the fireplace is a well-bal-
anced grouping of chairs, tables

KEY: (1) piano and bench, (2) davenport, (3) book table and lamp,
(4) pull-up chair, (5) wing chair, (6) end table, (7) over-stuffed chairs,
(8) drumtables, (9) tub chair, (10) desk and chair

RIGHT

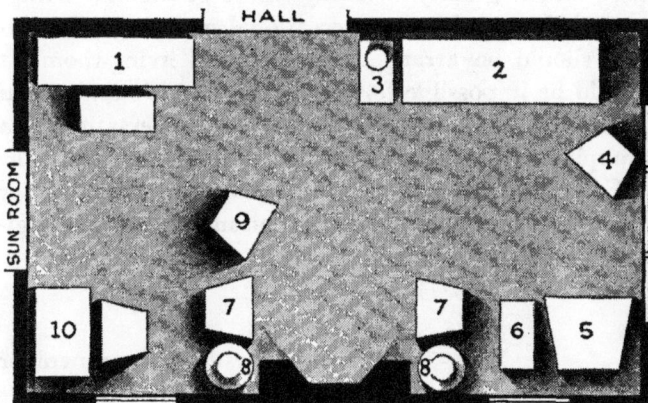

No matter how roughly your plan is sketched, it will give an impression of how your rooms will appear when finished. A scale of one-fourth inch to a foot is convenient. In this way you may measure the larger pieces of furniture and know beforehand what space they will fit on your plan. If you are building a house of your own and already have your furniture, plan with your architect the placing of the various pieces, keeping in mind the type and size of your furniture.

Put Plans on Paper

Paper plans allow you to place furniture and shift it about without the tiring physical effort of actually moving everything when you wish to try new ideas. With furniture well placed, a room should complement the lives of the family that use it, expressing in its arrangement of beauty and comfort the taste and interests of its occupants.

For hospitality and sociability it is wise to plan the arrangement of a few movable chairs about the room. This is where the small table, stool, and other pieces have added greatly to the comfort of modern living-rooms. Two or three conversational groupings of furniture should be arranged for the ideal living-room. It should be impossible for anyone to find himself seated alone in a room unable to join the conversation in a grouping that is just too far away from the solitary chair.

Certain rules apply to furniture arrangements. After they have been complied with you may carry out original and individual ideas.

ONE of the first rules to remember is that the important pieces of furniture should always

A charming arrangement of formal balance, attractive in any room, has been achieved here in the furniture groupings and the location of the pictures on the wall. This is an ideal way of hanging small pictures

be placed parallel to the lines of the room. Pieces such as sofas, large tables, pianos, heavy desks, beds, and chests, placed diagonally in a room express restlessness and are distracting, throwing the whole room out of line. This same rule applies to rugs.

INCORRECT

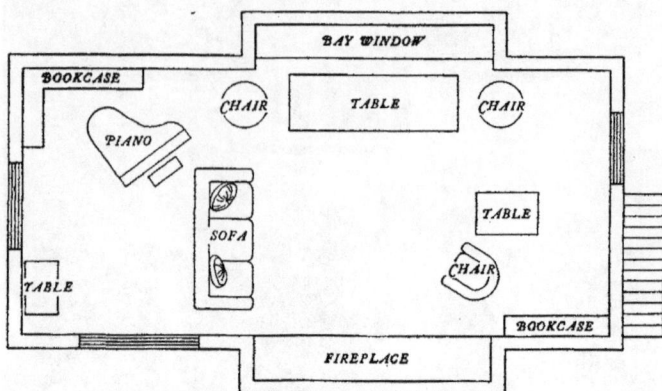

THE two diagrams above illustrate what is incorrect and correct in the arrangement of furniture in an oblong room. In the first diagram you will note that free progress across the room is awkwardly interrupted; also that the balance in arrangement of furniture is out of proportion. The position of the piano does not follow the lines of the room and the result is distracting. In the diagram

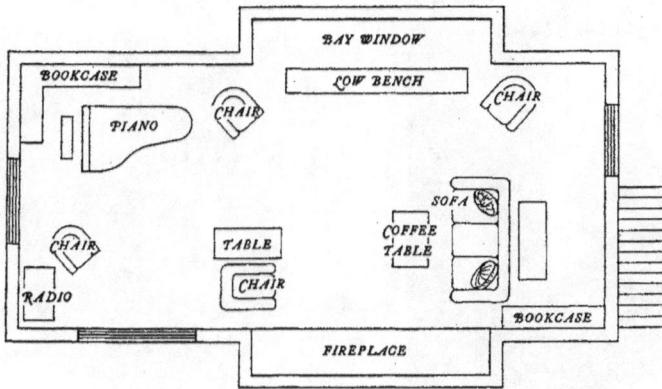

at the right, showing the correct placing of furniture, the floor space thru
the room is clear, and the piano is in an
infinitely better position, while the
sofa, placed on the other side of the
fireplace, succeeds in balancing the
effect of the piano. There is little
contrast in the arrangement shown
in these diagrams, but enough to
show how greatly arrangement fig-
ures in a room's appearance.

A pleasing version of informal balance. With the door in the center of the wall, variety is obtained by filling the wall space on each side of it; yet there is balance in the result

The relation of furniture to wall space must be made according to balance. If you have a paneled room the large pieces of furniture must be placed in the center of the panels. Order in the arrangement is essential to a room. All passageways should be left clear so that in passing thru a room you will not have to go around furniture.

Centers of interest should be left open. This includes fireplaces or bay windows where the view is to be enjoyed. Place your chairs or sofas with a definite idea of their use; if they are particularly for reading, then

An ideal fireplace grouping may be achieved when the sofa is placed by the fire with a large comfortable chair opposite it. In this photograph the mantel arrangement is formal with the furniture grouping informal. Incidentally, this is an excellent example of modern furnishings Direct, simple, and entirely without affectation, the style gives the room a distinct individuality, with the interest centered about the attractive mirrored fireplace

When a small room does not permit a sofa,
chairs may be drawn up to the fireplace comfortably as pictured here. This is a particularly
good grouping for Early American furniture as
it obtains attractive effects with the corner
bracket, the prim little silhouettes, and the rug

good lighting should be near. If the sofa is primarily for
rest no lights should shine in the eyes of the person
seeking rest.

Furniture pieces that can be ideally grouped are
sofas, with small tables at the ends, or a low oblong table
in front; two chairs, one high, one low and comfortable,
with a conveniently low table between; a smoking
stand by a deep comfortable chair, and an easy chair
by a piano or radio.

When a room is small it is wise to plan leaving the
center of the room free, for it gives the sense of added
space so often needed.

The placing of the sofa away from the fireplace,
against a wall space, is often advisable when a
room is small. It aids in enlarging the room. The
sofa is ideally located in the picture shown
here. The new cover on the sofa smartens it, and
the occasional table and white chair combined
with the screen make this an attractive grouping

A clever idea in a room's arrangement is to place the desk with its end to the wall so as to break up the straight lines about the room. The desk and two chairs are of maple, and the two Godey prints on the wall have maple frames. Note the way in which these pictures are hung, giving balance to the grouping

The idea of the small table has become one of the most practical notes in the modern arrangement of furniture; so much so that the card table grouping forms a permanent part of a room's arrangement as illustrated here

When drawing your furniture into your floor plan, first of all decide on the center of interest in your room. In most homes it is the fireplace, or it may be a bay window or a group of windows with a view, or the interest may have to center in conversational groupings.

In small rooms without a fireplace, place your various groupings toward the center of the room. Many rooms suffer a monotony thru having the furniture all too

In a gardened-home sunroom, flowered chintz
chairs can be comfortably grouped. Note that
the plants are placed so that they do not ob-
struct the view into the garden. Care in the
selection of wall covering, flooring, and curtains
and a little thought given to the arrangement
of the furniture have resulted in the charming,
hospitable room pictured here

much the same in height. This makes for an uninterest-
ing room. High pieces in a room are equally as important as low.

Such pieces as secretary desks help to furnish a wall
and carry their design and color up. This is where wall
hangings of chintz or heavy shawls or tapestries are a
great aid.

WE offer you many suggestions of furniture arrangements in our photographs, but you must not follow

any one of them blindly. Gather inspiration by placing your own pieces as the family needs them or as your guests may unconsciously pull them up when they have dropped in for an informal visit.

The few simple direct rules we have outlined will help you to begin your furniture arrangement. Obey them because they are fundamentally necessary, then fill in with your own ideas.

Do not strive to be conventional or go to the other extreme by posing as unnaturally original. True originality is as a rule born of necessity and is most attractive when it develops in this manner. If you would

For an unusual effect, place your knee-hole desk endwise to the wall and arrange a wall grouping like this above it. The extra stool gives balance to the entire plan

have your home more than a hotel in atmosphere then turn your thoughts to expressing your own ideas.

In the home that has the happy faculty of expressing ease of arrangement there is the feeling that everything has just fallen into place; but you will discover that deep knowledge and thought have been given to such a room and that the charm of atmosphere has not been achieved in a hit-or-miss fashion.

A sturdy stool beside the comfortable, well-lighted chair will serve as a table or as a seat for the story hour

OTHER SERVICES

Color in Your Home . . . . . .   20 cents

This is the newly revised edition of this
popular service booklet—solves many a
troublesome color problem and gives
many new color combinations.

Well-Dressed Windows . . . . .   20 cents

Important suggestions for the selection
and making of curtains and draperies.

Table Settings for Every Occasion . .   25 cents

A beautiful booklet of correct table settings, well illustrated with photographs.
Revised edition.

Floors, Walls, and Ceilings . . . .   20 cents

Detailed suggestions for finishing new
floors, walls, and ceilings as well as prac-
ticable ideas for doing over old ones.
Recently revised.

Bride's Book . . . .   25 cents

Whatever your part in preparations for a
wedding, here is concise advice. Also
shopping aid for the new home.

My Better Homes & Gardens Baby Book . . $1

This handy, daily child-care guide begins
with prenatal suggestions and supple-
ments your physician's advice until baby
is 6 years old.

Send required amount in coin or stamps to

The Home Service Bureau

BETTER HOMES & GARDENS

Des Moines, Iowa

www.ingramcontent.com/pod-product-compliance
Lightning Source LLC
LaVergne TN
LVHW041239080426
835508LV00011B/1285